Literature written for young adults...

by young adults.

Allow yourself to be surprised.

I0835551

The Star Gazer

Young Writers Chapbook Series

Ava Wong

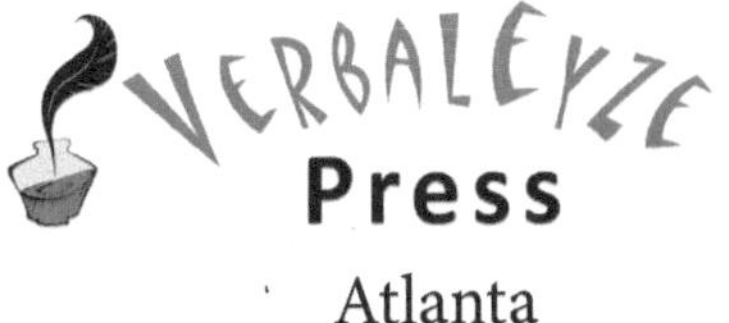

Atlanta

Published by VerbalEyze Press

Cover design by Ava Wong
Edited by Derek Koehl
ISBN: 978-0-9910209-5-9

VerbalEyze Press books are available at special discounts for bulk purchases in the United States by corporations, institutions and other organizations.

For information, address VerbalEyze Press, 59 Thayer Avenue SE, Atlanta, Georgia 30315.

VerbalEyze Press
A division of VerbalEyze, Inc.
www.verbaleyze.org

Table of Contents

The Star Gazer

Foreword

Every teacher understands that those who love the craft are perpetual students.

While mentoring, teaching and guiding the YaHeard? Poets, I have become their student venturing to type poems into smart phones and opening my mind to Instagram as a viable canvas. They want to keep me current. And I still insist that they meditate on Rilke's *Letter to Young Poets* and put pen to paper every now and then because this is an exchange of ideas.

As we explored the many ways to express our place in the world, we realized that word and art were beautifully intertwined so we made room at the table and became the YaHeard? Art Collective. The name was simply a formality. Young artists avail themselves of every art form as they test and train their unique voice to ask the questions, challenge the status quo and confirm their presence as artists on the come-up.

So it is my honor to introduce the aspiring photographers and visual artists who dared to illustrate the growing pains their counterparts recorded. Each art form confirmed the other as the writers marveled at being understood and the artists beamed at being able to interpret what was unspoken. This is certainly the beginning of a beautiful friendship.

And this collaboration is what the art community is all about. Come and see for yourself what has been sketched, narrated, painted and poeted.

Whether speaking heartache at the mic, spitting social commentary over tracks or texting observations into the ether, the power and influence of word is undeniable and the

YaHeard? Art Collective studies the craft, explores the creative process and revels in collaborations with organizations like VerbalEyze—a beacon for young artists.

YaHeard? was founded by Educator-Artists to support the creative stirrings of tweens and teens and the publication of this chapbook honors and encourages the work of a young artist whose passion and talent confirms them as part of a new generation of prolific writers, artists and photographers.

Open your heart, ready your mind and take note. The teacher is ready to begin.

Ya Heard?

Susan Arauz Barnes
Co-founder
YaHeard? Art Collective

Editor's Note

VerbalEyze Press exists as an extension of VerbalEyze's simple mission to develop the next generation of great authors and provide those young authors with a platform from which they can share their vision and passion.

The Young Writers Chapbook Series is an expression of this mission and vision that is core to what we do at VerbalEyze. Through this series, we are able to introduce talented, emerging young authors to the reading public.

We are grateful that you also share an enthusiasm for young authors and the vibrant and energized perspectives they bring to our shared understanding of the human experience. Despite their young age, they speak with insight as to what it means to live, long, love, lose and wonder as we travel through this world.

With this edition of the Young Writers Chapbook Series, we are pleased to bring to you *The Star Gazer*, the début publication of an exceptional young writer and artist, Ava Wong. We trust that you will be as engaged and challenged by her words and art as we have been. Ava is part of an exceptional group of young writers and artists, the YaHeard? Art Collective. She and her fellow writers are an never-ending encouragement and inspiration to us.

Read, enjoy and, as always, *allow yourself to be surprised.*

Derek Koehl

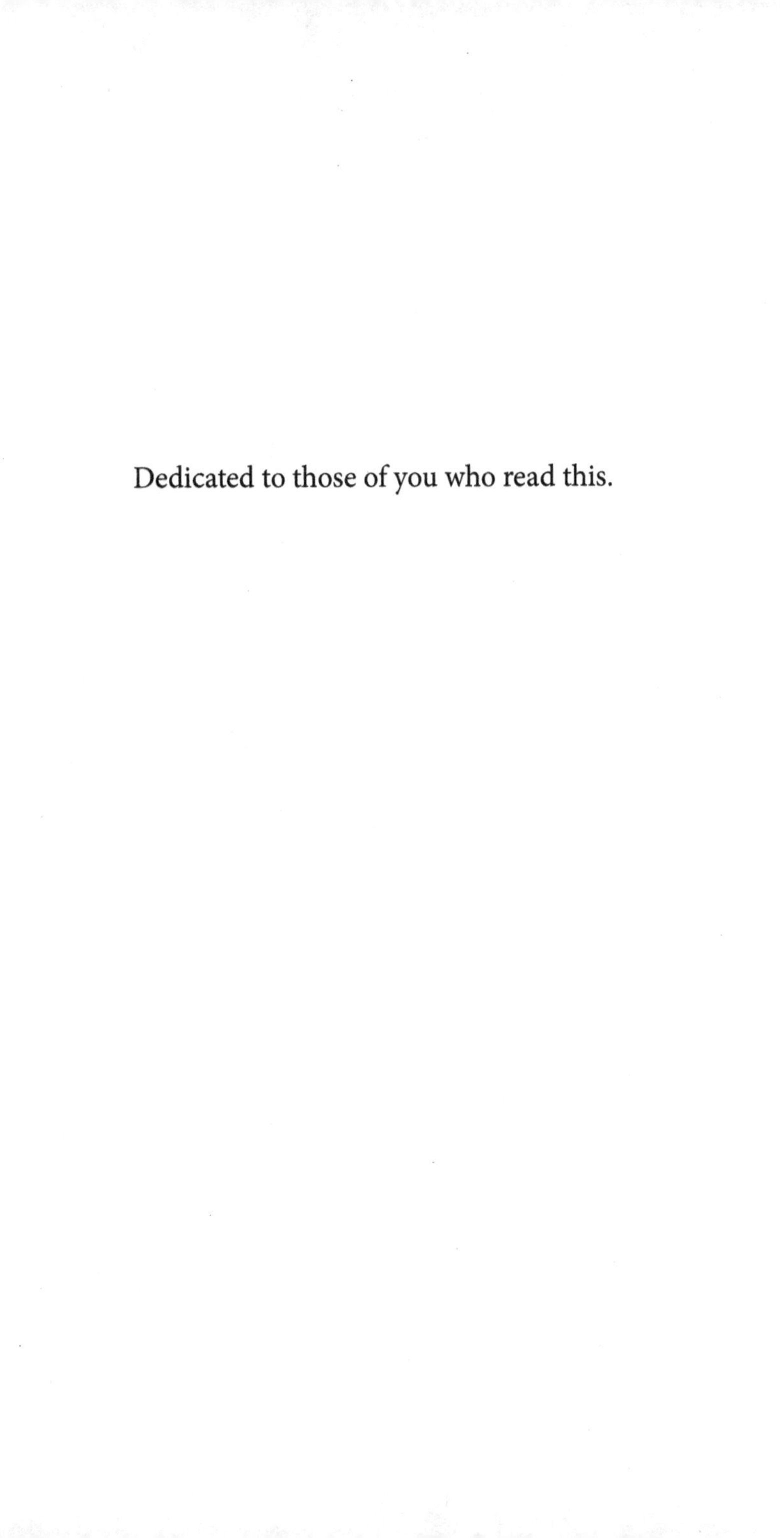

Dedicated to those of you who read this.

Route 66

For
Four
Long years
Tears
Streaked
Down my cheek
You traveled down
Her careful back
Long years fighting
To be here
Such a dear
You are finally near
Tears
Of fear
Are no where
Near
Here
Because she brought you here
Safe from war

My good ole'
Route 66
Dear,
I've feared for years,

The Star Gazer

You may dodge left and not right
You've made it home
Everyone so proud
You've made it home
Without even a scratch

Ava Wong

Cotton

Soft and damp pale clouds
Cradle my head
Singing me
Lullabies
Moon shining
Lighting the sky

Hummingbird

Dew in the morning
Calls pea sized wings to fly out
Of protecting branches

Ava Wong

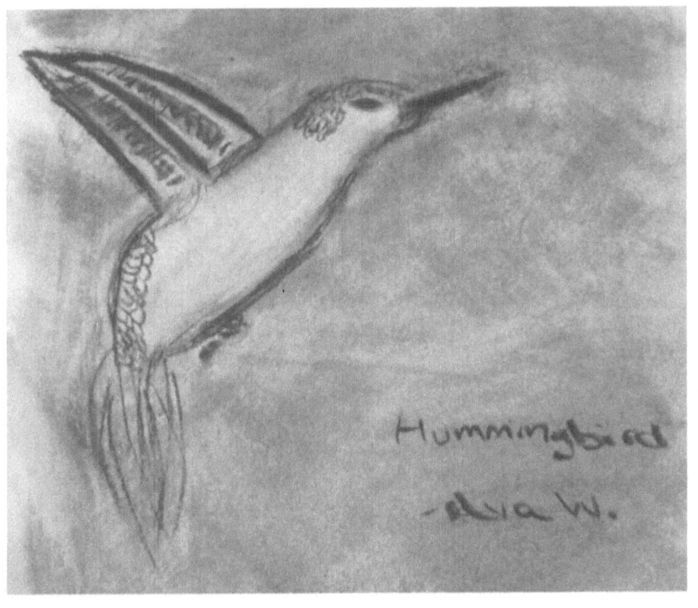

"Hummingbird"
Charcoal on sketch paper

The Headless Horseman

Anger strikes down like lightning
His story no longer a myth
Pain pours over my cheeks
Drip-drop
Drip-drop
Suddenly by the gallons
Dark droplets splash against cold stone
Winds whirl
The murderer dancing in
A dramatic telenovela
Darkness and evil lurk
Creep in like the black clouds above
Wind carries them swiftly to me
Bolting down like a baseball pitched
But at least the sun shines when you play
You sense his presence without seeing or hearing him
He has arrived.

Ava Wong

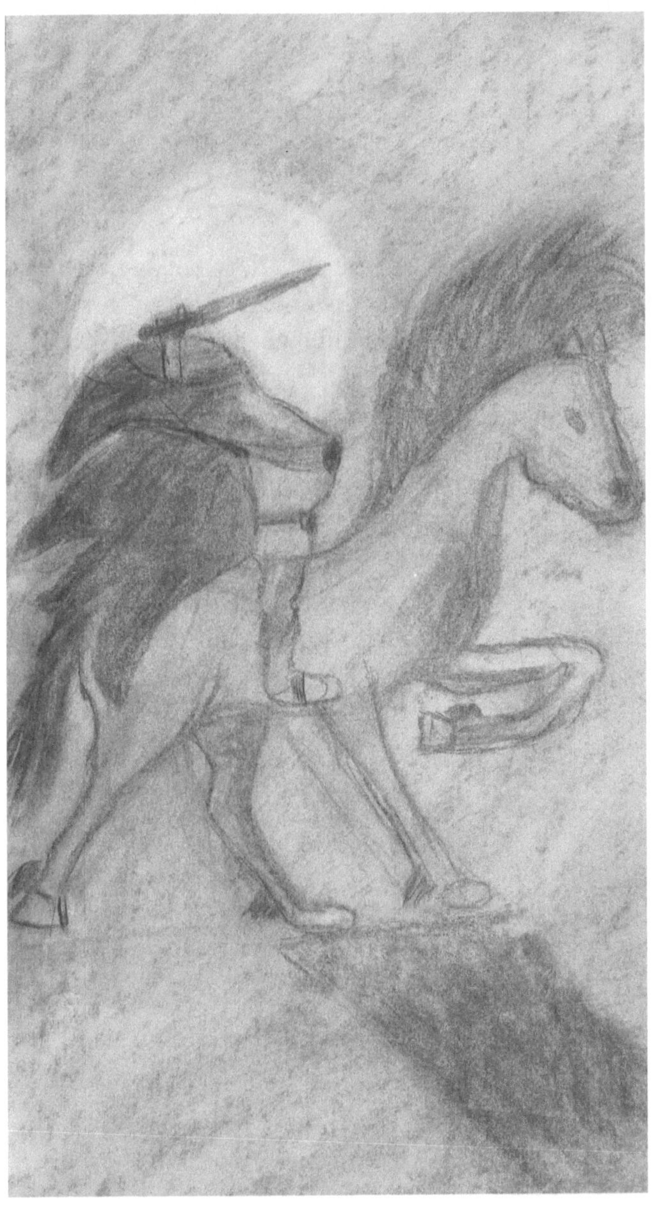

"Headless Horseman"
Charcoal on sketch paper

Depth

His story

His eyes stare into the dark depth of angry storms and sad clouds raining sins that is his life. From a family of four, he wonders how long God will make him wait to have a place called home. No rest, no sleep,

"No emotions allowed in war but strength," says his captain. No dreams, just hope. Killing off those called evil and protecting those called good with his shield of iron.

Eyes lay easy on the wall of the memorial, but for veterans, a wall of souls lay beneath the cold stone.

Ava Wong

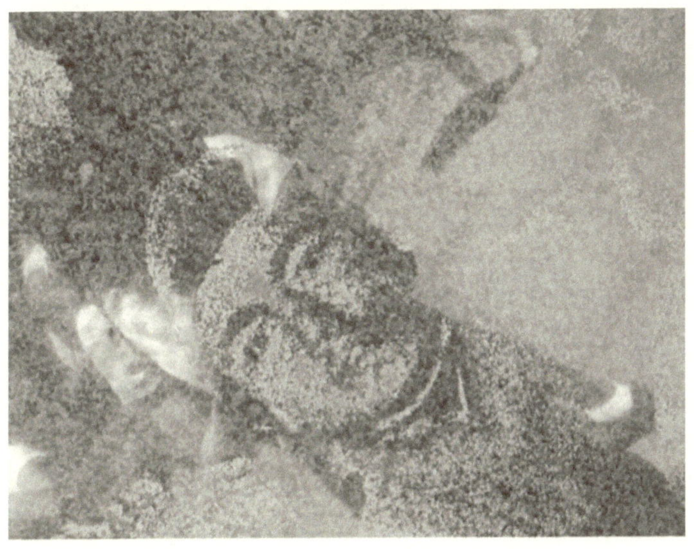

"Man of Depth"
Korean Memorial
Washington, D.C.

Keys and Locks

Locking me out of my dreams
Keys open treasures and sometimes a lesson:
Sometimes things are locked for a reason,
Not to be seen.
Dark hollow cases
Small enough for my hand to hold
Scarier than what Pandora did.
At least she saved hope
And there's something in my chest
Found in a tomb
On a Mexican island
Buried thousands of feet under
Never to be seen
A door in the way
Of my heaven
Those singing lollipops, dancing gum-drops, skipping candy canes

If I only hadn't lost my key

Ava Wong

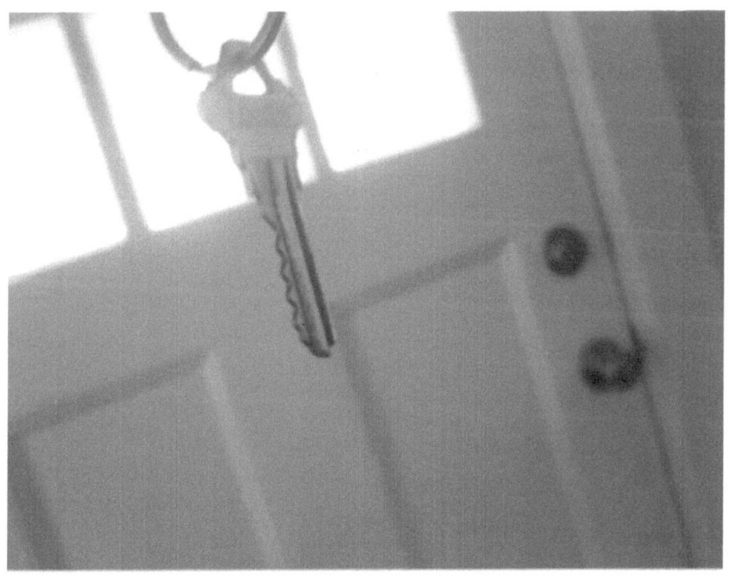

"In My Way"
Home in Atlanta, GA

Without Any Clouds

Howling at the moonlight
Darkness arise
A man's best friend
Wild as can be
Mark the territory between you and me
Fighting for food and shelter
It's just their life
Head of the pack
No going back
We're not alike anymore

But sometimes, when the tide rises just right,
And clouds are blocking anything from you and me
I see the stars and think of you.

Ava Wong

Free

Writing my own fantasy
Being what I can be
Using my gifts
To help others with their fantasies
As high as the clouds in the world of Narnia
Send me to Gallifrey
Meet me on the planet Raxacoricofallapatorius
I wanna bike for my birthday
'Cause that's my fantasy
Everything is going drastically,
Help me hold it back from thee,
Before they get me,
Save the dre—

Uncapped

I'm uncapped
There's no stopping me
I'm on a roll
Down my hill of dreams

I'm an agent with a mission
I could hack into anything
I feel free
Uncapped,
There's no stopping me
Don't close me up,
'Cause I got somewhere to be.

Ava Wong

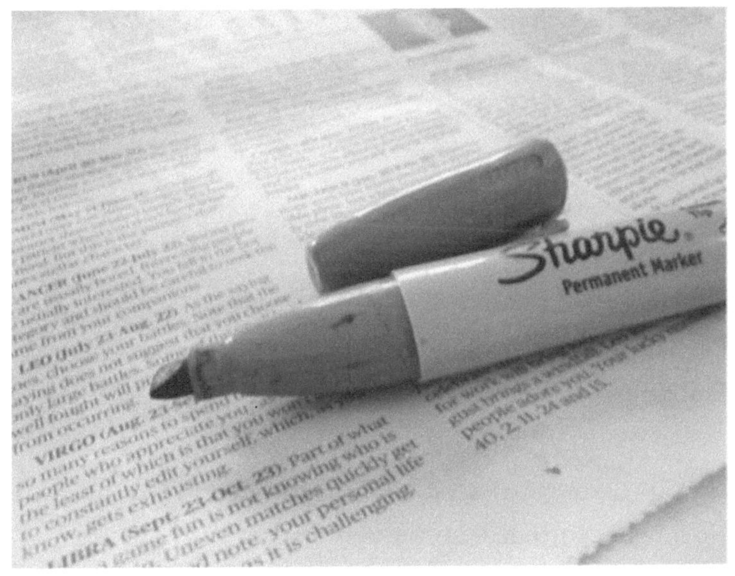

"Uncapped"
Kirkwood, Atlanta, GA

Buttons

Don't push my buttons
I've got a short temper
Don't slide the right one
And don't touch the left
I'm controlled by my buttons
So no one wants to befriend me
First day of 2nd grade
I'm controlled by my buttons,
Embarrassed even by Ms. Sutton

Now on my way to high school
No longer controlled, my buttons,
So don't mess with me.

Ava Wong

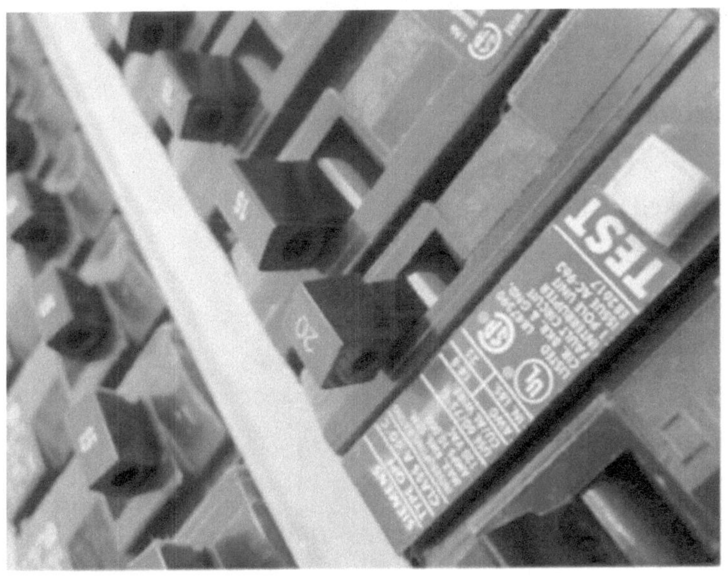

"Controller"
Home in Atlanta, GA

Stacked

Stacked up by bits and pieces
My life
I'm too busy talkin' like Yoda
It's like no-duh
Stacked up like newspaper
Each word is a story in my short life
A day in my catastrophe
The clutter in my room
The grammar mistakes in my newspaper
Can't nobody even see me up here
Stuck in a tree, help me
No one can't hear my cry of help and not each a laugh as I tell a joke
And it's not like I can climb down
I got my life in danger
But my life in a danger
They need to make caution signs for just me
My mind buzzing back and forth just like a bee
Trapped in a cup with no way out.
Just like me.
Higher than can be
Stacked.

Ava Wong

"Stacked"

Kirkwood, Atlanta, GA

Fantasy

I thought my life was just a fantasy
A story
Lined with pages and daring edges
Of mountain sides I climbed
Written by the master of all words
The mighty God
Apparently
I've been told
That the heroes in our stories
Are only heroes
If we
The pages makers
Find them true enough to be
Heroes
The ones with the sword and the majestic horse
Or the quiet ones sitting on mushrooms
Who save the day by accident
Or now-a-days
The buff ones with a gun and an agent ID.
I thought this was my fantasy
I was living my dream
But it turned out to be
What I can't be

Ava Wong

The Dove Held at Gunpoint

Shot dead in the middle of No Man's Land
Killed somewhere near the head
Basically ripping him open
Sickened by the pain felt through the letter
My father no longer
My mother crying
Brother sternly asks to move on
At age 16, as tall as can be
Wants to go to war
With the British, you see.
Apparently, God made him to fight for his country
And family
I'm in 1st grade
My teacher, Ms. Kinley
'Spose to be looking for friends
Not how to spend
The little money we've got
Left after war
I tell my now small family
No more to war
They both call me a pacifist
Whatever that might mean

The Star Gazer

I just want my father home
Telling stories by the fire
Keeping the food fresh, money safe
Eyes permanently wet
Red in the face
A scar you can't replace
Over your whole face
No more hope in the air
Brother packs his things
A little black bag
Like the hole in my heart
Sorrow brushes us in the wind
The train engine wails
It doesn't want to leave either.
The wheels creak
Smoke arises
Only a waving hand says good-bye

Ava Wong

The Star Gazer

Before the hopeful light died
I was a gazer
The only one of my time

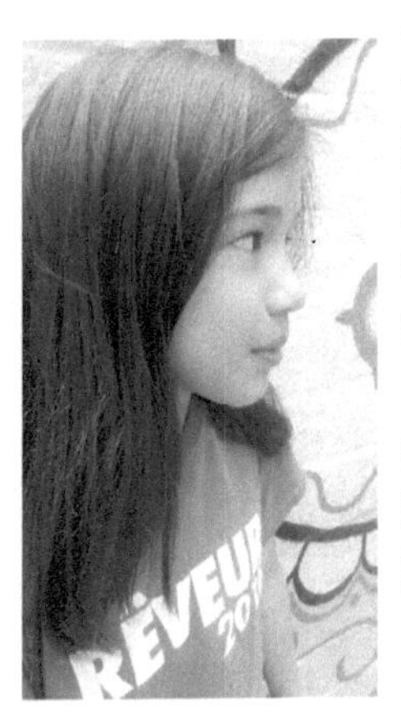

At age 8, **Ava** knew writing was what she wanted to do. Ever since she met Ms. Barnes, her amazing 6th grade English teacher at the Ron Clark Academy, she decided that she would do anything to be on the YaHeard?Art Collective.

Ava enjoys writing, sketching, and photography. She has always dreamed of writing a book and currently, you are reading her first!

Photo credit: Susan Arauz Barnes

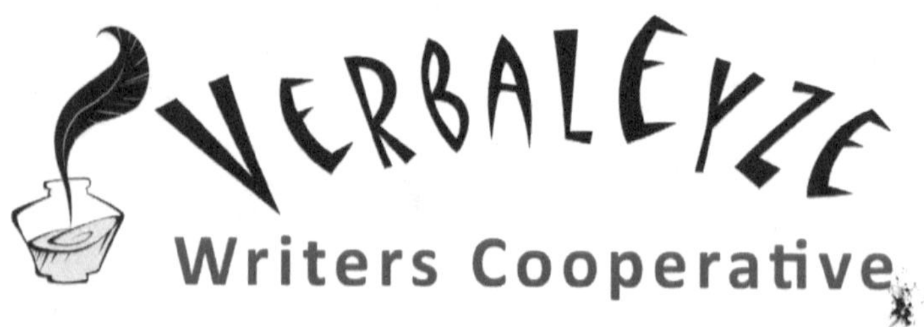

VerbalEyze is a nonprofit organization whose mission is to foster, promote and support the development and professional growth of emerging young writers.

The Young Writers Chapbook Series is published as a service of VerbalEyze in furtherance of its goal to provide young writers with access to publishing opportunities that they otherwise would not have.

Fifty percent of the proceeds received from the sale of the Young Writers Chapbook Series are paid to the authors in the form of scholarships to help them advance in their post-secondary education.

For more information about VerbalEyze and how you can become involved in its work with young writers, visit www.verbaleyze.org.

www.ingramcontent.com/pod-product-compliance
Lightning Source LLC
LaVergne TN
LVHW041929090826
845145LV00017B/2752